Annemarie Eveland

Real Women Don't Wear Glass Slippers

Annemarie Eveland

Library of Congress Cataloging-in-Publication Data.

Eveland, A. 2015

Inspirational Stories.

ISBN-13-978-1512321456

ISBN-10-1512321451

Real Women Don't Wear Glass Slippers

Copyright C 2015. by Annemarie Eveland.

First Edition.

Manufactured in the United States of America.

All rights reserved. No other part of this book may be reproduced in any form or by any electronic or mechanical means including information storage and retrieval systems without permission in writing from the publisher, except by a reviewer who may quote brief passages in a review.

Design for book cover by Annemarie Eveland
Book cover Art by Deb Schwalm

DEDICATION

This book is dedicated to my family
-the one born with me-
and the one birthed from lasting friendships
I adopted along my path in life.

CONTENTS

Acknowledgments

Introduction ix

Chapter 1 Redwood Giants Teach Truth about End of World 1

Chapter 2 Bear Encounters Wonder Women 5

Chapter 3 Water Nowhere But When I Needed It 16

Chapter 4 Where Are The Elk? 23

Chapter 5 My Favorite Christmas 29

Chapter 6 Coastal Highway Reveals Face Of Christ 35

Chapter 7 The Flagstaff Dig 41

Chapter 8 Utah Camper Saved By A Deer 45

Chapter 9 Manly Guys Pose With My Big Fish 53

Chapter 10 Master Learns Humility From Her Dog 59

Chapter 11 Chaco Challenge 65

Chapter 12 Story Poems 71

Other Books 99

About Author Annemarie Eveland 101

ACKNOWLEDGMENTS

I am grateful to the women in my life from whom I have received strength and courage to deal with challenges in my own life.

These women, sister-friends, are not just a source of joy and support, they are shining examples of how to handle life's toughest moments with grace and determination.

With appreciation also to my friends author Connie Cockrell for her assistance in the layout of this book and to Artist Deb Schwalm for her art work on this book cover.

INTRODUCTION

In our lives, we tend to take our daily events pretty much in stride, but as we reflect upon the deeper learning that each of them offer to us, we can glean some meaningful treasures.

When we review our lessons in life with curiosity and openness, we are expanding our strength, our willingness to be flexible and to see a bigger picture. We grow ourselves.

Often, it is in our real moments that we find new meaning and purpose. It a very simple experience, but often clues to spiritual fulfillment are nestled in the little aha moments.

Here are a few stories from some of my days I am pleased to share with you with hopes that they will bring a smile, a chuckle or maybe even an acknowledgement of a worthy learning.

CHAPTER ONE

REDWOOD GIANTS TEACH TRUTH ABOUT END OF WORLD

*"Some believe it when they see it.
Others see it when they believe it."*

This story shows how our illusions can control our beliefs and set in motion powerful learnings. And how I learned something worthwhile from nature and from younger people.

I rented a cabin deep in the Santa Cruz Mountains of California to escape my hectic weekday work in San

Francisco. One weekend I drove down from the city to my little hermitage in the redwood forest.

Fresh smells of pine needles always brought a smile. I breathed in deeply, sighed comfortably on the exhale, and walked to the back deck of my cabin.

I was thinking about my new friends, a young couple who had been married only about six months. They spent all their money faster than they could make it, going deeper in debt and nonchalantly saying, "We only live once; let's live it up! Everything will work out."

I must admit, I was a little incredulous and secretly critical about their momentary fun-life. I was raised with so much emphasis on saving and preparing for the future. We were very judicious about using monies for practical needs, not frivolous things.

I gazed out at my redwood giants. These trees were spared being cut down because the deck was built around them. I sat down on the deck and opened up my current book to read.

It wasn't my personal choice, but I promised my friends I would read cover to cover the predictions of Nostradamus. Predictions of gloom and doom and the ways the world would shortly end.

Soon, I was engrossed in his lurking legacy. The cataclysmic upheavals of the world graphically described the earthquakes and other tragic events. The graphic predictions caused me to shudder.

Suddenly, as I was reading about these shocking predictions, the ground began to shake and shudder.

I was tossed back and forth with the undulating upheaval. The forest before me began weaving back and forth in a blur.

I was stunned! *Incredible, I thought that I am just reading about our world fate and here it started happening...at least a major earthquake for California!* I began shaking. Panic raced through my head. My heart beat faster. I could hardly breathe.

My first reaction was to run. Run to safety somewhere. But where? I realized there was no way out. I couldn't get *anywhere* safely. In the next breath, something curious happened. I accepted as my fate, my death.

If there was no place to run, no safety net, nothing I could do; then the best thing would be to accept "what was." I silently reassured myself that my safety was not outside of myself, but deep inside where my spirit would survive.

So, I breathed in deeply, and on the out-breath let go of all my struggling and expectations that I would live through the next moment. I then experienced a profound, peaceful calm.

With that inside peacefulness, I noticed something peculiar. In my eagerness to find my escape, I had leaned forward and now everything was still, silent, and ...then I discovered that my entire experience of the big "final earthquake in California" was an illusion caused by my leaning against the redwood tree which swayed quickly back and forth in the gusts of winds, so naturally I swayed too.

I burst out laughing at the ridiculousness of my illusion. Then, I saw another deeper truth.

I had made my peace within myself, believing the great destruction of my world had come, and therefore even death was a place of peace for me.

And now, "resurrected" from my own illusion, I could laugh at myself but be thankful for knowing that it was my *belief* of what was happening that helped me deal with an issue that is very real for all of us humans- our fear of death.

I thought about my young friends who lived moment by moment, and promised myself to add a little more balance to my life. I would be more spontaneous and frivolous; as though it was *my* last day to enjoy earth.

I sighed with relief and hugged my teacher, my redwood tree, as it continued to dance with me. In my newly found courage to face my own death, I realized that *real women don't wear glass slippers.*

CHAPTER TWO

BEAR ENCOUNTERS WONDER WOMEN

*"Courage is not the absence of fear;
it's taking action in the face of it."
Author Unknown*

I did not know what lesson I would be learning when I accepted my friend's invitation to hike in the beautiful Sequoia Redwood forest.

As with life, if we knew what we would be experiencing in the future, we may be reticent to take the plunges. Sometimes it is our innocence or our ignorance that saves us from ourselves.

"You'll definitely need these." The Park manager looked somber as she pointed to the heavy black canisters. She plunked two steel cans on the counter with a loud thud. Kings Canyon National Park in California lay in the beautiful Sierra Nevada mountain ranges where my friend Jenny and I planned to backpack.

"And you're going to need to sign out *and* back in when you return." Her dark brown eyes flashed with authority and grim finality as her lips tightened into a straight line.

I squinted against the light streaming through the overhead window and tried to read her expression. *Surely, it's just a suggestion,* I thought. But, her laser gaze again pierced through me.

"I really don't understand what the big fuss is about," I protested. "We're backpacking into the wilderness for only three days. Gosh, I've solo backpacked in the Colorado Highlands for weeks at a time without armored food holders."

Partly frustrated, definitely fatigued, low on emotional reserve because I had flown from Arizona with all my equipment, shopped for staples, organized a navigation route and arrived late at the park lodge where my friend worked as a tour guide in Sequoia National Park.

"I will show you the most beautiful place to go hiking." Jenny had promised.

Good enough for me, I thought. Besides, my friend Jenny was whispering in my ear, "We don't need *those heavy, black things.*"

I faced the brisk bulging green uniform across the counter again. "Forget these canisters. They'll be too bulky. Our packs are already heavy. I figure if we eat a lot, we might lighten them some the first day."

Ms. Park Major replied, "Well, I can't force you to take them. But it *is* bear country and you will have to sign (yes, you guessed it, still another piece of paper) a release form stating they were not responsible for anything that would happen to us.

With a flourish I whisked the paper off the counter. My pen scribbled illegibly on the designated line. Then, as Jenny imitated my dancing signature, I saw a flicker of impudence dart from her eye.

We turned and bid our quick goodbyes. Then we heard Park Mama say, "Don't forget you *are* going *into* an environmental area, so everything – and I DO mean *everything* – you take IN has to be carried out. Remember the slogan? Leave nothing but footprints!"

A certain edgy smile marked her lips as she punctuated each word carefully. Almost as if she was casting some sort of a feeble spell upon our trek.

"No problem!" we both chimed cheerfully and departed feeling somewhat victorious for no apparent reason.

Parking at the trailhead with heads held high, we set an energetic pace down the trail. The giant Sequoia trees like monumental ancient centurions loomed overhead.

Layers of forest leavings blanketed the trail making our footsteps quiet. The air was cool and soft. Only an occasional twig snapped underfoot and the gurgling of my shifting water bottles broke our silent walk.

Late afternoon grew long with dark shadows. Warm sunlight filtered through the forest trees, casting magical sunbeams onto the forest flora floor. Occasional sounds of unfamiliar bird calls pierced the silence, but I saw none.

A storybook setting. I expected to see a fairy or at least a leprechaun jump out from behind one of the tree trunks.

These trees, these old giants of long ago have heard footsteps over thousands of years and conversations that no other person could witness.

Perhaps it is fitting to find them standing as a symbol of longevity and dignity to ages long past our usefulness or understanding.

My rumination was cut short when my hiking buddy suggested we take a break. She noticed a ledge which overlooked the canyon and I nodded that would be a perfect spot. We both loved panoramic vistas.

Soon, we dangled our legs over the ledge. I reached down and pulled off my boots. Now, any worthwhile backpacker knows how wonderful it feels to get hot sweaty boots off for a little fresh airing. The only thing better for feet is a cool mountain stream to soak them in. But for now, ah, that cool breeze blowing around my ankles and feet was heavenly.

And that million dollar scenery – the great expanse of row after row of mountains, the verdant greenery of evergreens and the brilliant blues of the skies. Wow! Who could imagine anything better?

We settled into the silence while staring at the breathtaking scenery.

Suddenly a loud Snap! Snap. Crunch. Snap!! We both froze. Only our eyeballs moved as they searched for the source of this startling intrusion.

Startled and dismayed, we spotted a huge brown bear lumbering down the mountainside. He looked like a fat bowl of Jell-O inside a giant fur coat. Lumbering and roly-polying along. His giant paws made thudding sounds as he came down the hill and onto the trail we just left.

It was about then I thought, *what in the world was I thinking? I have just cut off any escape route. Here we are, dangling on the side of this cliff and nowhere to go, but down, down, down!!*

I swallowed hard. My eyes still fixated upon the bear which loomed bigger as he loped closer. He loped purposefully along the trail and then to my utter amazement, he bypassed us and headed down the trail. I noticed a large curious thick black band around his neck.

As he disappeared in the distance, I exhaled a deep sigh of relief. Jenny said, "OK, I guess we can go now."

Said with such calm, I thought her to be a most impressive brave wilderness woman. I was still secretly shuddering.

I pulled on my hiking boots, double-tied them and stood up only to find myself a bit woozy. *Not the altitude for sure*, I thought. *I surely don't want to meet that fellow on our trail again.*

We hiked up the trail for a good hour. I began to feel the tiredness in my legs. The sun was dimming with dusky pre-night sounds. Crickets, hunting birds, squirrels were around and other mysterious night sounds became noticeable.

I suggested we find a suitable spot for a campsite to rest and regroup. She agreed. We climbed uphill off the trail, and I murmured, "Fat furry" won't be back the same way."

Half way up the mountain we found a semi-level spot for our little dome tent. It was then I recalled the Park Momma's words... "Bears...food...we take no responsibility." *Ah...yes, better get food out of our tent and away from our sleeping place.*

I collected all food sources and bagged them in my new Gortex gadget bags, color coding them for "breakfast, snacks, dinners, etc." Then I tied several bags to each end of a three foot rope.

Scouting the hill I found a long tree branch and with all my bags in tow, walked down the hill, selected a tall tree and hoisted my food packs over a high limb.

As I stood back and surveyed my secured stash, I smiled smugly. Surely no bear could ever reach up that high to the limb where I had tossed my food bags.

We trudged uphill to our safe rip-stop nylon security hut for a good night's sleep. As both of us snuggled down into our sleeping bags we heard sniffing, loud and close.

Sniff. Sniff. Snuffle, Sniff.

In the dimming light, we read the fright on each other's face. I held my finger up to my mouth signaling "Shhh!" We dared not breathe or for sure not move a muscle.

The sniffing continued. Likely, only a few seconds more, but in my head it felt endless. Suddenly, silence again.

We waited and waited, and when my straining ears could no longer detect any movement outside, she whispered, "Has *IT* gone?

"Whatever IT was, IT is gone," I said softly. "Now, let's get some sleep. I am tired." We both turned over and back to back, went to sleep.

We were awakened early the next morning, not by the light surrounding our little nylon castle, but by more sniffing, snuffling and grunting.

We blinked awake, frozen in movement again. But this time, because of the bright morning sunshine, I saw a huge shadow hovering over our tent.

More rustling, and sniffing and grunting. Then, the big shadow pawed the ground and shuffled away. We waited to exhale. The silence was deafening.

Finally Jenny said, "Why don't you go outside and see what it is?"

Incredulous! I thought. But then I also thought— What *What kind of real protection is this flimsy piece of nylon tenting anyway?*

I listened again for those sounds which petrified us. Nothing.

Finally, I gingerly slipped on my hiking boots, pulling the laces snugly at the top and double knotting them. My thinking at that moment was simple— *Don't want them coming loose when I am running for my life.*

Softly, quietly, carefully, trembling a bit, I unzipped a tiny crack of the tent, which revealed only a slice of morning light against the pines.

I braved another inch or two, so my two fingers could part the zipper. *Still ok.* Now I became very brave. I unzipped enough for my head to stick out. Still ok. Nothing around.

"Well, that is *enough* of this timidity," I told Jenny. With one long determined downward motion, the entire flap flung open. I stepped out onto the forest ground and looked around.

Still, only the quiet of the forest and the beauty of the morning light greeted me. "Come on out, Jenny," I exclaimed. "All is well."

We both stood outside our tent and stretched. My gaze went downhill, way down to that tree stash. I gasped.

There was waddley giant brown bear with his fat black collar. He had gotten my Gortex bags of food and was rolling around on the ground pawing and licking and chewing our food.

I was outraged. How dare he shred my new Gortex bags. They cost me plenty. Then came a moment of sanity.

"Jenny, we have to get out of here fast. This is a dangerous situation." I began quickly dismantling tent and stuffing everything into my backpack.

I was fully packed, yet she was still standing there slowly putting her camp items together. To my amazement, she didn't appear concerned.

It was at that point, she confidently said, "I hear if you rush them they run."

"What!?" I hissed. "You gotta be kidding! That's crazy."

She took a few more precious moments to convince me it *was* true; she worked at the park and talked with the rangers.

Somehow, she convinced me it was the savvy thing to do.

A few moments later, with full packs on our backs (minus of course all our food) we each clutched one end of my bright orange plastic ground tarp and raced downhill towards this bear shaking my tarp while screaming and yelling at the top of our lungs as ferociously as we could muster, "Grrrrrrrahhhhh!"

As we got very close, the furry Jell-O bowl looked up in surprise; then ambled up on all fours and turned and walked behind some large bushes.

"See, I told you," Jenny said with some air of confidence.

But then Jell-O bear cocked his head to the side, as if to say, "Nay, I don't think so!!" and proceeded to come back in front of us.

Instantly, I grabbed my Nagene wide mouth bottle, quickly unscrewed the top and shook the apple juice vehemently on the ground before him.

All the while, I whispered to Jenny, "Back up slowly and quietly and don't say anything."

Fatso Brown Bear plopped onto the ground and began licking the apple juice up with relish, making sloppy moaning sounds while he licked the ground.

When we were back far enough, I turned and said, "We have to run before he comes after us."

I remembered it was Jenny who told me bears can smell 800 times more acutely than humans, and I still had apple juice on my hands from shaking while I poured it out.

"Come on, Jenny. Run. Run," I croaked. And I turned and ran as fast as I could. The first stream we crossed I drenched my hands in water to wash off the smell of the apple juice I would never drink. I could see Jenny trailing behind me.

We ran. We ran until we reached my car, parked at trailhead. My legs shook violently. I braced myself against the door to open the lock. My hands couldn't hold the keys. It took two times to get the key into the door.

By the time I opened the door, Jenny was on her side. We both sank into the car's safety and I was going to rest a second before turning on the ignition, so my legs would stop shaking, but she said, "I have seen at the park where bears rip off the doors of cars to get to the food."

I shoved the key into the ignition and we bolted out of the parking area. *Glad I backed into the space when I came here to park.*

We raced back to the park headquarters in silence. I was mulling over our backpacking adventure...so far. What took us three and a half hours to briskly hike in, only took us one and a half to run out. Not bad motivation.

I broke the silence by saying, "You know we have to go back there and get all that mess that bear made with our stuff...remember Park Mama warned us when we chose that environmental area? We both sighed, thinking about facing Jello bear again.

Back in the safety of park headquarters, we learned there was a nuisance bear. A big brown nuisance bear who had raided camps and had attacked hiker. They had collared him and were tracking him and going to move him out of the park for the protection of visitors. Maybe his name was Jello Bear.

I had mixed emotions learning about our bear. Shucks, it was his territory before we came along and claimed squatters' rights.

Somehow regardless of my frightened moments in his presence, I felt sorry for him and wondered about his future.

And my final thought about our close call and the stamina it took to run from the bear? It reminded me my hiking boots *were* needed because *real women don't wear glass slippers!*

CHAPTER THREE

WATER NOWHERE BUT WHERE I NEEDED IT

*"Women are like tea bags.
They don't know how strong they are
until they get into hot water."
Message on a Tea Towel*

There are times in our lives when unexplainable things happen which defy our rational thinking. We have no way to explain it, and we struggle to accept it. But because these unexplainable events happen to us, we know them to be true. This was mine.

In life there are many circumstance that we are presented with as opportunities to grow. In this story I override my belief system that limits me for what I can do for a project, and discover a new freedom and appreciation for myself.

This was my first backpacking survival venture. The educational training was a seven day trek into the famous yet rugged Superstition Mountains of Arizona. Peter Bigfoot of Reevis Mountain School was leading us out on a trek. The trek tested what we learned in class of how to survive on our own in the wilderness.

The class consisted of all male students who easily fell in step behind him. I pulled up the rear. I was the only female on the trek.

I wondered how I was going to keep up with them for this week long trek. They all looked hardy and a lot more fit than I.

I had taken some healing courses at Reevis Mountain School for a while, and thought now I needed to learn how to survive on the desert, in case I got stranded sometime.

A simple decision in the making, but as we were going to plow into the thickets and down steep trails into the rugged wilderness, I questioned how sane I was when I made the commitment to go on the trek.

We were allowed one pound of food and one quart of water. That was it. We had to forage for everything we needed during the time we were out.

Peter went through our packs before starting, tossing many items out.

When he came to inspect my pack he frowned and quickly pitched my toothpaste, hair brush, any high energy bars, and on and on. I let him toss out everything except when he came to my Tampax.

"No!" I groaned. I envisioned myself having to make do with mullein leaves or worse.

"All right," he said with a slight grin on his face.

I glanced around on the ground now strewn with a colorful array of items forbidden to be put back into our packs. As we stuffed our packs with acceptable essentials, we faced our first day of hiking.

Soon we headed up the trail, Peter Bigfoot in the lead. His large feet (hence the dubbed named "Bigfoot") needed size fourteen shoes and in his true self-sufficient manner, he made his own shoes using tire treads for soles. His long gait was a challenge to keep up with, but I was determined to stay part of the pack.

I pulled up the rear of the trekkers. *How was I to keep up?* I pondered. These guys were tough and ready, and I was considered a tenderfoot. Then I devised a plan.

I would put mental blinders on and only see the boot steps in front of me. Where ever they stepped, so did I. If his boots slipped on that step, I sidestepped it.

Minutes turned into hours and then a rest stop was announced. To the surprise of some of the guys, I was still with them. And doing pretty well. I hid my smile but felt my hand patting my back.

Four days later we were getting very low on water. I kept having thoughts of digging holes or sucking on barrel cacti.

It was midday, the sun was fiercely beating down on us. We walked in silence (mouths closed to preserve our moisture) and my eyes scanned the bright hot landscape.

Then unexpectedly, I saw a shiny glint off to the left of me in the distance. I stopped and gazed in that direction. There it was again. Like a mirror reflecting just a hint of a glint.

I unsnapped my backpack, dropped it on the trail and walked over to the green Palo Verde tree which was about 200 yards away and stopped short.

To my surprise there was a large canteen—the old fashioned kind with fabric covering the sides of a metal round container and a wide woven strap. I must have stared at it for a few moments before I realized that it actually was a container for water.

The canteen was wedged into the crevice of the tree. I pulled it out and found it was over half full of water!

And when I opened the top and took a drink, the water was cool. *'How can this be?'* I thought.

Then I had another discovery. I saw a name on it printed in bold letters.

I recalled just before I was leaving home for the trek, my significant partner at that time said, "I wish I could know you will be okay. I wish there was something I could do to help you on your trek. "

He wasn't the outdoor kind of person, so I could not imagine *anything* he could do to be helpful.

Yet, there it was on the side of the canteen. His surname was definitely printed boldly in black lettering. Enough water to share with my fellow hikers, too. I was even more grateful for my practical find.

How that canteen was wedged in the Palo Verde tree, I cannot say, but I was reassured that day that all our real needs can be met—even when there is no water in sight.

I believe it, because it happened to me and showed me *real women don't wear glass slippers.*

CHAPTER FOUR

WHERE ARE THE ELK?

"Don't give up on your dream
because it is not going
in the direction you want.
There are different routes
to the same destination.
Author unknown

When I moved to the mountains, I had a dream. A dream of seeing those powerful and massive elk up close and personal. I tried unsuccessfully to get a glimpse of them anywhere. Then one day, I discovered them quite by accident.

This is the story of how my quest for elk taught me more than just seeing these powerful animals, but learning from them.

I was pretty much a city slicker when I first came to live in a small mountain village in the north central mountains of Arizona.

I locked my doors, dressed warmer than needed, was home before dark about and was careful to get a cultural city fix every now and then since there "wasn't much to do."

I also held a curious yet passionate search for wildlife, especially the elk. I had seen the deer and my heart leaped upward, but the lure of seeing a massive four legged furry beast with antlers extending into the sky was all too exciting.

I would ask, "Where are the elk? How can I see them?" An amused smile crossed the local faces. No matter where they pointed me, the elk did not arrive.

Finally it was explained to me that elk have their own paths, places and nocturnal times. They decide to come around when they want to. Elk can't be ordered up like a cup of Starbucks in the city.

Glumly, I resigned myself to the fact that I would be one who would have to look at photos or listen to other stories from those more fortuned to see the big guys.

One day when I came out of our little village market and went to get into my car, I saw a street sign along the highway that intrigued me. It read "cemetary" road.

I was puzzled by the odd spelling of the word cemetery, certainly different from my Webster's Dictionary. I am not ghoulish by any means, but I thought maybe it was named in the early days of pioneer history here when not everyone could get a formal education. I decided to investigate.

I headed up the dirt road which, of course, ended at the village cemetery. It was late afternoon and sun filtered through the trees, casting magical looking shadows. I stopped my vehicle at the gate entrance, opened my car door and stepped out.

I thought I saw distant statues of ...yes, elk! Then I mused, "What a community! These folks like the elk so much they made elk statues for grave markers in their cemeteries." Under my breath I whispered, "Hooray! These are *my* kind of people!"

Suddenly, one of the large statues moved. Then I saw four statues, all moving. These were the *real* elk with five and six pronged antlers, which later I came to properly call them "racks."

My heart raced excitedly. Leaning on the door frame of my vehicle, I wondered how I could get closer to them. I really needed to see them *much* closer. I didn't want to scare them. Not that these solid massive mammals couldn't handle themselves against a small object such as myself.

I took a few moments to study them, I noticed that one was always "on guard," watching while the others munched tender green morsels on the ground.

Then, by some unspoken signal, the guard would put his head down to graze and one of the others would take the watch. As this cooperative watch continued, I devised my own plan.

Each time their "shift happened," with my arms stiffly outstretched from my sides and my fingers spread wide, I took one large step forward and stopped immediately as the guard's head came up. I stood still, silently repeating in my head, "I am a tree. I am a tree. I am a tree."

Each time they shifted, I stepped one long step forward. Each time they stopped, I stopped, ever thinking "I am a tree." This process continued until I was more than half way across the cemetery, getting closer and closer to my ultimate goal, to see the elk close up.

Then an unsettling thought crossed my mind, "What if they came running towards me? What if I got trampled in their exiting?" There wasn't really anything to hide behind. I felt a rise of fear.

Even though I didn't move a muscle, the instant I had this thought, all the elk heads jerked up and stared straight ahead in my direction.

I drew a tiny breath inward and forced myself to relax. I repeated in my head, "I am a tree. I am a tree. I am a tree."

All four elk then went back to grazing, and I to my one-tree-step-at-a-time, getting closer to them one secret step at a time. Finally I stopped and just watched them graze.

Minutes ticked by, and then they turned, one by one, and as if by silent agreement, gracefully leaped over the fence and disappeared into the forest.

My own tree limbs shivered a bit as I saw how easily they could leap over the high fence from a standing still position. What magnificent powerful animals, I thought. What a memorable visit to a cemetery. And I was still standing.

Now I tell people, if you are looking for the elk, you might try looking for them in the late afternoon at the village cemetery.

You might see the elk or you might see me. I am the tree.

My cemetery adventure with those statues of elk satisfied my driven desire to see them. The live elk helped me remember that in taking chances to realize a goal, *real women don't wear glass slippers.*

Annemarie Eveland

CHAPTER FIVE

MY FAVORITE CHRISTMAS

"The best Christmas gifts in the world are not in the material objects one can buy from the store, but in the memories that we make with the people we love."
Amanda Boyarshinov

Holidays can bring out the best in people. This holiday was my chance to share the magic of the holiday season and bring out the child-like joy in my friends.

I devised a plan, and decided to take a risk and celebrate in a way that was dear to my heart— the magic of childhood Christmas. I know I received the greatest gift in the giving.

It was a chilly and wintry weather that holiday season. My mate and I decided to invite people who didn't have family for the Christmas holiday weekend and celebrate with us in my home in mountains of Arizona.

To share the holiday with others made it my favorite Christmas. And, yes, of course, they were delighted to come!

On Christmas Eve I gave each guest a stocking to hang above the fireplace. The grunts and polite groans were typical of humans who had become jaded and jangled by life's ever seasoning hardships. Not much of their cherished childlike candor was evident.

I was viewed as a "polly-annie." Yet, the stockings *did* have their names labeled clearly, so dutifully to please "polly-annie", they hung them by the chimney without much caring.

As everyone went upstairs to bed that evening, the winds blustered about boldly. When the "zzzzzz's" began, I tiptoed outside into night's cold darkness, cautiously and quietly taking each stocking with me.

I filled each stocking with goodies and hung each fat sock stuffed with whimsical items. Each child's handpicked Santa gifts nestled under the magically lit Christmas tree.

It was a seemingly long task begging my patience and determination. Finally all wrapped gifts snuggled under the tree and all their overstuffed Christmas stockings sagged heavily from the mantel piece.

Dawn cut thin slices of light over the mountain's ridge as I slipped into bed pulling the warm down comforter deliciously over my icy body. It could only have been a few minutes, but I was in deep sleep when I heard shrieks and screams!

I bounded out of bed, wobbling and reeling awake from thick-fogged headiness. I finally realized the sounds were of delight, not danger.

Our adult "kids" had found the magic of Christmas! Their first sounds woke the entire household. Then everyone else ran quickly downstairs.

Giggling with delight, they pulled their little toys and thoughtful gifts from Santa out of their stockings. Each little remembrance fit each little child perfectly. "How did Santa know I liked...?"

We watched "our children of this Christmas become reborn" and smiled warmly. Such transformation when believing in magic!

The gleeful eyes, the upturned mouths, the sounds of giggle in the key of happy, all added to our appreciation of what magical role we could play with them.

Later that day, I made midday fondue. Now fondue is an adventure in itself if it is your first attempt. My first trial was two different cheeses bubbling energetically in fat wine-laced pots warmed with fire and trays and trays of choices to dip— breads, veggies, and meats.

The finishing fondue was the experimental chocolate fondue, rich creamy, lots of sugar and even more, what was that, Kirsch? Whew. We all jabbered eagerly as we sampled lots of the dessert fondue. The more we ate, the fewer of us talked. The more we ate, the more all of us talked less.

Soon, our little beehive of conversational beings— about twelve or more— melted into silence.

It was then I began to notice, one by one, each curled in a cozy comfy spot in the living room away from the fatly furnished fondue table, and drifted into dreamland. Too much Kirsch? Oh, well, we will wake up....sometime. *So good not to have a schedule or agenda about things.....today,* I thought as I laid my head down too. Then all went dark.

Late afternoon, after our reviving naps, one by one the sounds of conversations began to rise in the air again.

I had invited everyone to bring something to share....it could be a story, a song, a life experience, anything they wanted.

My mate was always fantastic in getting people involved in activities, so he was our master of ceremonies. I always knew if he handled our crowds, they would be inspired and cooperative. So, everyone began to share.

One sharing stands out for me. Storywriter, Ellis. He wrote children's stories and wanted to read one for us. We are all up for that adventure, brought our pillows and blankets into the living room and curled up on the floor for a great storytelling legacy.

Ellis seemed pleased when he looked at our earnestly scrubbed and upturned smiling faces. "Once upon a time...." he began. Ellis read, and read...and read.

If he had not been so intensely involved in his entire presentation, he might have looked up and seen before he got much past the beginning, we were ALL fast asleep.

None of us heard his story. None of us heard anything...until that magic moment when he said, "and they lived happily ever after.

As if on cue, we all somehow woke up, and leisurely stretched. Some people yawned, but to cover our embarrassment at not hearing his first one, all of us said, "That was a fantastic story, Ellis! Tell us another one."

So, what could Ellis do, prodded by our eager encouragement and his own great ego telling him we loved his stories? So, he began again. "This is the story of a princess and.........." Again, our eyes closed slowly, while our storyteller went on his storytelling journey—alone.

Ellis devotedly told three stories from beginning to end. Now, it wasn't that his stories were not good (I read them myself later.) They were great!

Later, when fully awake, some guests said it was the generous overdose of Kirsch I put in the fondue dessert that made them sleep through all his stories.

I prefer to think it was so very nice to snuggle up with a "blanket and cushy cotton cloud pillow" while drifting into the magic of childhood storytelling. I figure we probably got our own versions through dreaming his stories.

When departing, each guest told me they were glad that I stuck to my dream to bring the childlike qualities out in them (and myself) despite their resistance.

That was the Christmas I did things *my* way despite the lamenting of my guests. Following my own desire to bring magic to the moment, I was rewarded with my own desired outcome and reminded that *real women don't wear glass slippers.*

CHAPTER SIX

COASTAL HIGHWAY REVEALS FACE OF CHRIST

"In order to move on in our lives, sometimes we have to accept that we might never understand what has happened. Some things are just meant to be a mystery."   Author unknown

At times in each of our lives, unexplainable things happen which defy our rational thinking. But since they happen to us, we cannot deny the experience and are compelled to accept it without explaining it.

One summer I lived at Big Creek Pottery Ranch near Santa Cruz on the pacific coast of California to study wheel-thrown pottery techniques. We didn't have electric kick-wheels there, only our legs kicked the large circular slab of concrete around and around for throwing our pots.

By the time summer ended, I could no longer get my right leg into my jeans, and had to cut the right pant leg up the side to wear my jeans.

Had I known that faded and ripped jeans would be popular now, I could have kept my two pairs of thread-bare jeans to recycle for my fashion statement.

The potter's experience was well worth it, though, as I was very happy with my clay creations. We also dug clay out of the local hillsides, and did Raku firing.

During classes that summer, I made a number of ceramic pieces for family and friends for Christmas gifts and several sets of dish sets for upcoming weddings.

To supplement my class and residency expenses, I created and sold enough of my self-styled pillows that summer to pay most of my expenses. I stuffed them with the foam crumbs, which required that I buy huge burlap bags of foam crumbs from my fabric wholesaler in Santa Rosa.

Since there was no class one day, I decided to drive up to Santa Rosa during the break and stock up on my foam crumbs for the pillow projects. I left early in pitch dark and drove straight through to the Santa Rosa warehouse. The burlap bags filled my convertible, and I had to leave the top down to cram them all in. Then I headed south again.

The trip seemed much longer coming back. Perhaps I shouldn't have gotten up so early that morning, but I was eager to return home to the ranch and get some more pillows made up for my customers.

After a while, the ocean lay below the windy cliffs. The twisting road required more driving effort than usual since I hadn't much sleep.

The Pacific Coast scenery is stunning and when I had extra time, I would use that highway rather than the freeways.

The warm sun, the whistling wind and glittering ocean reflections made me sleepier. I fought the fatigue with images of new pillow designs and loud music and with all my windows rolled down, let the wind whip through my hair.

However, that method didn't last long. After a while, I stopped fighting the fatigue and all went dark as I drifted asleep.

Suddenly, I was jolted awake only to see the ocean far below me and my car directed straight towards it. I had not realized that my car had veered off the proper lane and was headed to the edge over a cliff.

At that moment, I felt a rush of panic, then simultaneously, the face of Christ appeared to me. I still cannot explain how and why because even though

I was raised very Catholic, I had not practiced the religion for a very long time.

What I saw was a face of the kindest, most loving eyes and soft golden light that I have ever experienced. All I remember feeling is, *I'm home.* I have never felt such intense radiant love before or after that moment.

There are no words in my head or heart to adequately describe this experience. If it had not happened to me, I might doubt it could happen to someone else. I felt such peace and safety that I eagerly surrendered all parts of me to that trusted image and moment.

It seemed like the experience lasted "forever" and I felt suspended out of time. It was probably a split second in earth time.

The next thing I remember is hearing a tremendous thud and my head jerked violently forward and hit something.

When my eyes focused, I saw that oddly enough, I was entirely on the other side of the road. My car had not only turned away from the ocean, but had crossed the road to the other side and had gone into a ravine of a sort.

All was still, except for the people who soon rushed down the hill to see what had happened and later I learned no one expected me to be alive

I stepped out of the car, and surveyed the damage. I could see that the driver's side front fender had been crunched badly. Other than that, there was no damage.

"Darn!" I said with obvious irritation in my voice. "Now I am going to have to get that fixed and I have no insurance. Shucks!"

While I was still mulling over the expense of that fender, the highway patrol arrived.

They insisted I go to a hospital. I was even more upset. I had no medical insurance. They actually took me there after a powerful convincing discussion. My car, driven by another, followed me.

"I am just fine. I don't need any attention!" I repeated again and again.

No one listened to me. They said they had to check everything out. The x-rays showed me to be just fine, much to the amazement of all and the secret amusement of myself.

It wasn't until much later that I had time to think about that face of Christ which had appeared to me in that moment.

Chills came over me. I knew only *then* how close death had come to visit and how close the kindness of Christ also visited me.

I carry that image in my heart, and whenever I think of it again, I get chills up my spine. It still affects me, even many years later.

The experience helped me know I am never left alone. And that it is important to remember that one moment in time that seemed to last forever and changed me forever.

That sometimes when we have profound moments in our lives, we know that *real women don't wear glass slippers.*

CHAPTER SEVEN

THE FLAGSTAFF DIG

*"Time stands still best in moments
that look suspiciously like ordinary life."
-Brian Andreas*

In life there are many circumstances that presented to us as opportunities to grow. In this story I override my belief system that limits me for what I can do for a project, and discover a new freedom and appreciation for myself.

I had minimal archeological digging experience, but when invited to participate in the Flagstaff Dig in northern Arizona, I was thrilled to do any kind of work needed at the site facilitated by Dr. Jeff Goodman.

By the time we volunteers arrived at the current work site, the shaft and tunnel was finished. To reach the end of the tunnel, however, you had to climb down a ladder to the bottom of the shaft and then crawl the entire length of the tunnel which ran under a dry river bed.

I get claustrophobic in elevators. I hadn't bargained for being under the earth. I thought it was an open pit style dig. But I was excited about participating in this unique and important dig.

So, when the leader suggested I go down and collect samples, I swallowed in disbelief. But here I was, on a dig with *real* archeologists.

I wanted to appear cool and collected. So, I managed to eke out a cheerful but tentative sounding, "Sure."

Armed with sterile Petri dishes, dental picks and more, I began the long descent. With each step down on the ladder I felt like a reluctant miner descending into a foreboding underground pit.

My flashlight headgear bobbed up and down. Finally, I touched the earth. Solid. And then I peered at the tunnel.

Much smaller than I had hoped for. But no wavering or whining allowed, I thought.

Contracting my body into a little bundle, I began crawling along the inky black endless tunnel. The smell of dank moisture clung to me; the darkness invited my imagination to play tricks on my mind.

My jeans began to clot the dirt as I inched forward a little at a time on my knees. My boot toes scraping a trail behind me.

Finally, the end came into sight. However, it brought no real comfort, as it meant that my job had just begun. I had warned the crew above that I would be able to stay in the tunnel for a half hour.....maybe.

I took out my Petri dish, and scalpel and very cautiously began to flick out tiny pieces of charcoal to be tested for carbon dating. It was important work, I reasoned. With a stalwart mindset I was going to do the best possible job. This meant making sure only the carbon was collected. No contamination with other stuff.

My entire world became one tiny fleck at a time. One small deliberate gentle movement. One small beam of light emanated from my forehead onto my hands. Soon, I forgot about all else but my important task at hand.

At some point, I heard a voice from far away say, "Come on up, Ann. It's lunchtime."

I had no watch, but I was sure they were fooling me. No way could it have been even a half hour. So I continued to work. Again, the call for lunch came.

This time, I tried to move. I found I was locked in one position. My body wouldn't respond. After rubbing my knees, legs and hips, I managed to squirm around and re-orientate myself the other direction. Then at a slow crawl headed back down the tunnel.

Sure is a long way to crawl for just a half hour of work, I mused.

When I reached the shaft ladder I painfully unkinked my back and arms. As I dragged myself up the ladder into the blinding sunlight, a volunteer came to help me out, and showed me his watch. Twelve straight up.

Everyone was eating their lunch. I had been collecting for over three hours without any break. *How did I lose track of time?* I wondered.

Time didn't stand still. I did. In focusing on one thing, (the collecting of tiny flecks of charcoal) I quieted my mind. And my concerns about claustrophobia were gone also. I reasoned that I had a project bigger than my problem.

I realized as we are in our *now* moments in life, we transcend our tracking time, When we are totally immersed in our *now* moments we are not concerned about our imagined future fears or reacting from our baggage of past experiences.

It was a valuable lesson to help me remember it is our *now* moment that is a useful tool to help with life experiences.

It is the only thing we own and that honors us. In pushing through my perceived limitations, I found a new freedom and powerful awareness that I could do much more than I thought I was capable of. I found that *real women don't wear glass slippers.*

CHAPTER EIGHT

UTAH CAMPER SAVED BY A DEER

"Go to peace, not pieces."
A. Eveland

For most of us, spending time in nature is a relaxing and rewarding experience. The beauty and peacefulness of natural surroundings brings our own nature back into balance.

My road trip through Utah was no different. I found great pleasure camping and hiking on the drive back to Arizona.

One late afternoon I stopped at a campground to spend the night, thinking I would enjoy a campfire evening and leave in the morning.

I was not prepared for how the next day would challenge me.

I pride myself on my ability to be comfortable in the outdoors. I could solo backpack in the wilderness, canoe alone on the lakes of Arizona, and thanks to my wilderness training, I could handle a seven-day trek in the Arizona mountains without fears or trepidations.

I drew the line at rappelling alone, though, for dangling from a rope without hope of touching the ground safely kept me from venturing out by myself.

So, my trip through the Utah mountains with a stop in a campsite wilderness area did not bother me in the least. I even found it a little too civilized for my personal taste.

I would rather choose the environmental wilderness areas where you never saw another human or a touch of trash or other leavings, let alone a fire ring for campfires.

The Utah campsites were basic without tables, hookups or fire pits. That was just fine for me, but still there were the "arranged" spots.

Oh well, one must make some concessions for the city slickers who liked condo camping when traveling! I mused silently.

I settled for the last campsite – secluded and backing up to the forest. No one around, at least when I arrived.

"Good enough for me," I mumbled as I got out of my van and began pulling out my tent and gear and set up my camp site.

Soon, I had everything arranged "properly." I always set out an extra camp chair with jacket and hat on it – the old standby to make it appear that there were two of us, not just myself. And most likely, the public would figure it was a guy.

The reddening sun began to slip behind the mountain ridge, the night folded into a jet black backdrop with glittering diamond stars. When the campfire died out, I rolled into my sleeping bag. So lovely was the feeling of a down mummy bag. I slept soundly.

The next morning I stoked the fire and sat beside its hot welcoming flames, sipping my hot steaming coffee. While I munched on cold muesli with apple juice I mulled over my activities for the day.

I wanted to explore down to a lake supposedly some distance away, but thought I would first take a little jaunt up the hillside to the ridge for an overview look. I would only be gone a half hour.

So after dowsing out my fire, I bounded out, leaving everything behind me. It crossed my mind that I *should* take my Ten Essential Bag to always be ready for emergencies. But I rationalized that I was only going to be gone a few minutes. *Not to worry,* I mentioned softly to myself.

The ridge rose sharply, and I had to bushwhack around several outcroppings as I wound my way around the stubborn rock facings.

Finally, I stood on top of the mountain to survey the landscape below.

However, it was packed with barbed brush and thick trees. I could not see anything to identify where I was. My sense of direction was obviously lost. I began to feel uneasy.

I started to walk fast first in one direction then the other direction. But all I accomplished was disappointment.

By now it was almost late afternoon. Daylight was beginning to fade. It had taken a good portion of the day trying to get to the top. Not to mention my futile attempts to figure out where exactly I was.

I walked even faster now. The cool late afternoon air made me shiver, and I wished I had brought my jacket.

The daylight was fading quickly and long shadows prevented me from seeing any distance. I panicked and began to rush through the trees. After a while, I noticed my own footprints on the ground.

I groaned. I had been going in circles. My mind was clamoring, *It is getting dark. You have to get back to camp now. It will be freezing tonight! Hurry! Hurry! Get going! But, where?'* I thought. I don't really know which direction to go.

Then I recalled that one *must* sit down and still the mind when lost. I looked for a place to sit down to calm my racing thoughts and the stern accusations I was giving myself. I was feeling foolish and scared.

I saw a log. I slumped down on it and closed my eyes. I took a deep breath. Then I took another deeper breath. Calm filled me. Then I slowly opened my eyes.

I was surprised to see a deer standing before me in a clearing in front of a group of pine trees. I looked at the deer still a little bit stunned and said aloud, "Well, *you* are not lost. You know where you are."

Somehow those words amused me. I gazed at the beauty of the deer. She was beautiful but powerful. As we looked at each other, I sat still, and she stood motionless.

Moments ticked by. I felt suspended in time. Then, as if she read my mind, she turned and slowly began angling down the side of the mountain.

I thought, *Why not follow the deer?* The deer turned and looked back at me. I imagined it saying, "Why NOT follow me? I know where I am going."

I followed the deer, down, down, down the mountainside. The deer did not run away, but kept a distance from me that encouraged me to walk faster and follow at a respectful pace.

It was getting very dark and cold by now. Soon, the sounds of gurgling water awakened by senses. It got louder and louder as we approached the stream.

The deer stayed in front of me, until she reached the stream. Then she turned and looked back at me as if to say, "You're okay now."

I could barely make out her outlined body as she effortlessly jumped the stream and disappeared into a thicket.

I stooped down and drank a few handfuls of water and reassured myself that all streams lead downward. So, if I followed the stream I would eventually come to something and it most likely would be the highway into the campsite.

I followed the stream in the dimming twilight, picking up my pace as fast as I could without danger of tripping.

Finally as night was falling, I saw the highway and breathed a sigh of relief. When my feet hit the asphalt, my heart silently leaped for joy.

Soon a car approached, and I flagged it down. It was a sheriff's car. I was thankful to see them and asked the shiny badges to give me a ride. I did not notice the seriousness in their faces as they queried why I was afoot in the area.

"I just need a lift to get back to my campsite," I told them. Then I added a bit sheepishly, "I misjudged my day walk direction."

"Not today," said the heavy set one with a rounded Santa Claus style face. He huffed a little and continued, "It's too dangerous. No one is allowed in. The area is sealed off. We are evacuating everyone."

I was amused and thought it was a kind of mistaken power struggle. *What had happened? A deer got lose or something?* I amused myself with the thought.

He continued, "There is an escaped prisoner on the loose. We think he is in this area."

"Oh, please!" I pleaded. "I *have* to get to my campsite. Can't you let me get my van and camp stuff?" I did not think much could happen in this beautiful serene mountain paradise area. *The guy probably had been arrested for petty thievery or some other minor infraction of a blue law,* I thought to myself but said nothing aloud.

They agreed to escort me but said to make it quick and drove speedily to my campsite. The campsite still looked fine to me, but I said nothing as we got out and I started collecting my stuff.

"Hey, look here," the lean and tall other one said. "Tracks. He's been here." He reached in the car for the radio and another gun.

Suddenly the hairs on the back of my neck stood up. A cold chill ran down my spine. I shoved everything into my van as fast as I could, without care or thinking where anything was going.

"What did he do?" I shouted. My teeth chattered now.

"He is up for murder." came the reply from the rotund man with the badge.

I couldn't move fast enough. My legs were wobbly and my hands shook as they grabbed whatever they could find.

Being murdered in my campsite dashed my idea of having security from a second chair at the campsite. Now it gave me no hint of security at all.

The sheriff's deputy helped me load things. In a few minutes that seemed to last for hours, we finally had me packed to go. One offered to drive me out. I humbly and gratefully accepted the offer.

I probably couldn't have focused on the windy road anyway. Besides, I did notice that my legs would not stop shaking. Didn't really matter now, as I saw my hands were shaking also.

We got to the highway in lightning time. They drove me to a small town nearby. I was so relieved to have them with me or more honestly, me with *them* and back into a more civilized environment.

That night, I stayed in a motel, grateful for the city surroundings. I would not say I slept soundly, but I did think a lot about how I took that walk that got me lost, how the deer led me down to the stream that led me to the highway and the sheriff.

If I hadn't left camp for that little walk, would I have been at the campsite when the prisoner came through the area? I shuddered.

Sometimes when we feel we are doomed, we are possibly being saved from something far more devastating. I was thankful for my unexpected angelic care that appeared when I most needed help.

This time possibly my angel was disguised as a deer. But most certainly it showed me, *real women don't wear glass slippers.*

CHAPTER NINE

MANLY GUYS POSE WITH MY BIG FISH

"Bragging may not bring happiness but no man, having caught a large fish, goes home through the alley."
Author Unknown

I love adventures, especially when they take me to places that I have not yet visited. So, when an invitation came to be the photographer for a group going deep sea fishing, I jumped at the opportunity.

It was a great time for a paid vacation and time for playing with my new camera equipment. I was delighted to learn that the famous researcher Jacques Cousteau and his crew on Calypso were also there on a filming project. So, I said "Yes!" very emphatically.

It couldn't get any better, but I was to discover just how much better it would get on this two-week fishing expedition.

I love the outdoors, but fishing? Fishing has always been a sport that I classified somewhere between men and wilderness. It came under the banner of odiferous smells, slick and slimy tactile sensations, worms dangling outrageously on strings of nylon.

Not to mention the disconcerting flopping of a dying fish with an eye staring at me accusing me of its demise. Yuck!

So, when I was invited to photograph a two-week marlin fishing expedition at Cabo San Lucas in Baja, Mexico, I had some reservations. However, the lure of also getting to photograph the natural beauty of Baja overcame my hesitancy.

I arrived at the hotel at Cabo armed with two large bags of camera, lenses and an array of filters and with my individual agenda.

My imagination whirled eagerly as my mind visualized my camera catching flaming sunsets or serene silver-spun ocean scenes.

Our first evening sunset did not disappoint me. It displayed a surprising colorful spectacle of ruby reds, flaming oranges and golden streaks melting into the horizon. I was breathless as I snapped one photo after another.

Early the next morning twelve of us boarded our yacht extraordinaire with its elegant amenities, including an authentic Italian chef and impeccably dressed captain and crew.

Eager to discover the great ocean with its waiting marlins, we set sail early. Several seasoned fishermen took their places, outfitted with fat reel holders, swivel chairs, huge reels and determined faces. When the captain found a good spot, they cast their lines.

"I'll take some candid shots and any other shots you request," I announced politely.

My announcement was met with comments from fisherman Jerry, "You'll have your work cut out for you, Annie, as I am well-known for catching trophy fish. So, how are you going to photograph all of mine and all their catches too?"

He smiled broadly, showing a perfect row of capped teeth.

The day wore on, without anyone catching anything. Our first day became longer overnight. Some of the hopefuls turned to swapping fish stories.

One futile day turned into six more long empty days. Still no fish caught to photograph.

The captain pensively tried all his favorite fishing haunts to no avail. Nothing. Everyone was getting edgy. Their quiet fishing lines hungered for any bite. Talk turned to past trips when they caught huge fish.

Finally it was January 21st – halfway into our fishing trip. Somehow someone found out it was my birthday.

"Hey, its Annie's birthday today," he said. Why not give her a line for a while? I accepted the opportunity, as I had never tried marlin fishing before.

I relished the idea of just sitting in one of those official looking fighting chairs. Maybe someone would take my picture too?

I smiled and climbed into the chair, took hold of the reel and rod as they snugged up my safety belt.

At this point, everyone laughed. It did seem funny that after six days with not a fish in sight, securing me into a bolted down chair seemed like overkill.

Maybe they were also amused with my awkward novice way of holding onto the rod and reel.

Minutes ticked by. Fifteen minutes seemed like an eternity. I started to say, "Okay, now I know what it feels like. Get me out of this chair. I'm done."

Suddenly a deliberate, quick tug on my line caught my attention. There it was again. This time it shook the line and my hands vigorously. I braced my feet against the side of the boat.

"Hang in there, gal," one of the men shouted.

My line zigzagged back and forth wildly, diving up and down.

Several men began shouting out their advice: "Give her line! Reel in. Let it out. Hold it tight. Don't let go! It might take you an hour with his baby! She is a tough one. If it tires you too much, I'll take over for you."

I took a deep breath and thought, *this is my fish and I won't let it go…to anyone else.* Suddenly my fish jumped out of the water in a perfect arch and it looked like it danced on its tail.

The marlin's blues and silver sparkled brightly in the sunlight. A loud splash and it went down into the water again. It took all my strength to continue reeling it into the boat.

A few minutes later, I got it close enough for the crew to gaff him onto the platform. *Wow!* I thought. *This is fun. No wonder they like to deep sea fishing!*

We all rushed to the stern to admire my catch. I wobbled back to see it. My feet bracing against the boat made my legs like rubber.

There in shimmering brilliance was *my* marlin. It looked huge! I started at the beautiful creature with pangs of guilt for causing its death. His large eye stared back at me as if to say, "Why me?"

Fish look different when delectably served at an upscale restaurant – without the eye!

More sun-soaked days of bright blue skies passed, with predictable flaming sunsets, followed by star-studded dark nights. Still no marlin.

Only the birthday girl's catch lay iced in the hull. Some of the guests looked glum, some were silent and others talked about having lots of margaritas with their dinner that night.

Then the day came to port back into Cabo San Lucas. One man said, "Annie, you are going to have to get your photo taken with your fish, you know. It's tradition."

So when we docked, I had my photo taken – my fish dangled tall and long beside me while I looked adoringly at it. The sign documented my catch. It weighed 104 lbs. caught in 20 minutes on a 30 pound test line. And by me!

Enough, I thought, *I don't need to go marlin fishing again!* I wondered what to do with such a huge fish. It was enough for me that I took the risk to try fishing and to actually land such a catch myself.

"Does anyone want my fish?" I asked as I departed the yacht. One guy was quick to respond.

"Yeah, I want to have my picture taken with it."

Other fishermen chimed in, "Yeah, let's do it."

"It belongs to you guys," I said and I turned to go up the hill to the hotel. As my feet trudged gratefully up the beach towards the hotel I glanced back.

Yep! Just as I thought – each man was having a photo with my mighty marlin.

I chuckled. I wondered what kind of big fish story they would be telling their friends back home about the catch.

But then again, it wasn't "my" marlin now. I smiled and murmured to myself— *real women don't wear glass slippers.*

CHAPTER TEN

MASTER LEARNS HUMILITY FROM HER DOG

*"Slow down. Calm down. Don't worry.
Don't hurry. Trust the process."*
Alexandra Stoddard.

We can learn from many sources. This story is about a lesson my little rescue dog taught me in the Tonto Forest. He reminded me of the futility of trying to control situations in our lives.

The sun shadows were long, stretching through the tall pine forest. It was late afternoon. I called out again to my dog disappearing into the pine forest. The tenor in my voice tight and highly charged. "Pine Buddy! Come here. Come on! Here are little treats for you!"

On the distant hillside amidst the pine forest, perched upon a fallen huge jack pine tree, I could see him still erect like a forest sphinx.

His black long face and cropped mini-pincher ears were upright as he stood regally surveying my frustration with what appeared to me as a mix of amusement and pride.

My gal friend had suggested we take our dogs to the forest near our Pine village. We drove up Hardscrabble Road, pulled off-road and let them out to run free.

I had some reservations, but spurred on with her reassurance that she did this *all* the time and her dogs come back so mine would follow them.

Wrong. He came back at the end of the "freedom run" just long enough for "hot dog return treats," then disappeared. Now, two hours later, I was still trying to get him in the car.

"Let's just head back," I said in resignation. "Maybe he will follow and get tired."

This novel idea came after trying everything else. I began driving away, straining for a glimpse of him in my side mirror. He stood still. "Come on, come on!" I thought pleading silently.

Suddenly, he jumped off the log, came running pell-mell down the hillside, catching up with my car speeding down the dusty curvy mountain road. "He's coming!" I pronounced with excited surprise. "Let him get tired first," she volunteered. Those next five minutes felt like fifty.

Then I said, "Let's stop for him. Stop we did. Stop he also did. I put treats, water, toys and myself on the road, but nothing could entice him to come close and get "caught."

Each time I reached out when he got near, he would run away. Every time I drove down the road, he followed close and stayed in sight.

"He likes this game," my friend volunteered in explanation. She added, "I've been searching for our local "Dog Whisperer" but can't find her. *She* could tell you how to deal with dog delinquency."

I differed from her take on things. I didn't think much of his game. I didn't want to leave him in the forest, for fear of getting lost or becoming dinner for a hungry mountain lion.

Daylight was fading fast. I looked towards heaven and used my usual lament for situations like this, "I could use some help here. Send in your angels."

As I finished my invocation, I saw a car kicking up clouds of dust as it came uphill. There hadn't been any traffic all afternoon. The woman driver pulled aside my van and asked, "Need some help?"

I was so relieved to see her, I blurted out unabashedly, "My dog is back there and won't get in the van. I don't know what to do!" I knew I sounded pitiful. I thought:

But, what could this little wisp of a lady do to help me with Pine Buddy?

She smiled. "I'm Lori," she said simply. "Let's see if I can help. I'm a dog trainer. I stopped suddenly. That seemed like important information, but I dismissed it as I was so focused on getting my dog back.

She told me to hold onto my dog's empty lead. Then she got her two dogs out of her car, and invited my friend's well behaved dogs to join the circle.

Soon, it looked like the storyteller's private canine counsel of the Hound Table.

I secretly glanced over at my rambling rogue buddy. Cautiously, he started down the road to see what was happening, circled slowly and came up behind me.

'My new trainer' said, "Do nothing until his head is in front of you." Eventually, Pine Buddy nuzzled his head under my arm and peered curiously into the pack conference. I easily snapped the lead on his collar. *Gotcha!* I thought.

Then, as if on cue, we all stood up, said goodbye and as we left, Lori gave my friend her card— the Pine Dog Whisperer's business card.

As I gratefully drove home, I commented on the coincidence.

The incident reminded me that frequently my reason for going somewhere isn't my only purpose for being there.

I thought we were taking dogs for a forest run, but it turned out that I learned a lesson in letting things unfold in their own way, and the bonus was finding the Dog Whisper!

Many times when we try control life situations we fail miserably; but when we give it up, and gently allow things to happen in their own way and time, we are rewarded beyond our expectations.

I laughed at my own discovery and jokingly said to my friend, "Maybe that is why they could call dogs, woMAN'S best friend."

At any rate, with our fur kids to teach us and keep us humble, I was reminded *real women don't wear glass slippers!*

CHAPTER ELEVEN

CHACO CHALLENGE

*"Life only demands from you
the strength you possess."
Dag Hammarskjold*

The power of nature at times brings out of us the undiscovered power within us. When we are faced with challenges in life, often times we discover our new level of strength. I called this one, my Chaco challenge.

Situated in the four corners area of New Mexico are the remains of an ancient civilization so vast during the height of its reign over hundreds of years it was the hub of civilization. Even today it leaves one breathless when looking at this archeological site, the largest in the southwest.

Our adventurous archeological group from Arizona went to visit. I was intrigued by this thriving culture from thousands of years ago. Major center of ancestral Pueblo culture. The major civilization for hundreds of years. At its peak over 100,000 residents and roads stretching out vast in all four directions; a hub of activity and the place for spiritual practices.

The landscape even today belies understanding. Its many ruins hold stories yet to be discovered. After visiting several ruins, we set out to the top of the mesa to visit another special ruin.

To climb to the mesa high above, we wedged our way through a small slot canyon, twisting and turning and using hands to pull ourselves up through the small openings. We goat climbed along rock faced walls to the top.

Atop cliff side dramatic views of vast landscapes and many ruins lay below us. We walked by worms fossilized millions of years ago still embedded in what was an ocean's bed.

The rock formations were startlingly ancient also. Each one held some secret of the past. From the mesa top, we set an energetic pace to Pueblo Alto, another ancient settlement near the north road.

Only a few minutes into our trek, raindrops began falling— faster than we were walking for sure. It soon turned into a downpour with thunder shouting and clapping around us. Determinedly we plodded onward.

At one point, the pelting rain turned into stinging pea sized hail. The unrelenting hail storm was fierce, blowing us about indifferently.

We took refuge and huddled under the only visible small juniper tree jutting out from the craggy rock face. We were unable to see beyond our own boots. The storm was brutal and foreboding.

A half hour seems longer when you are huddled in a tiny space to diminish blowing rain turning into side wise pelting hail. The relentless howling wind forced us to stay huddle together to wait out the worst of it.

When it eased up a little, we trudged determinedly onward, splashing through the rain dotted mud puddles and slip sliding over clay ground. The drenched ground made it precarious each step. Rain and hail turned it into slick mud much like skating on ice.

The thick terracotta mud clumped to my hiking boots, making hiking even a bigger challenge. I was drenched completely even with my rain suit on.

The man leading us down the mesa was over 80 years old; spry and sprightly he nearly danced down the mountain. His stamina and ease of fast paced hiking despite the conditions was amazing to me.

I wondered how I would keep up with him, but was determined to get out of the thrashing rains and pelting hail storm.

So, I pulled my hood tight around my face and watched his every step — slipping and sliding and tromping down we went past footholds in the rock face that the ancient ones used, past the noteworthy ruins that were hardly visible now behind the sheets of hail.

One step at a time, I told myself. That is all you have to do. Just one step at a time.

Finally we came back to slot canyon and descended partly on all fours, partly by just seat sliding down,

Of course, when we arrived down at the base again, the sun came out to greet us.

When we returned to camp, piles of hail clumped to the ground and my tent's rain fly shredded, so the tent filled with water. Another reminder of the power and control of mother nature.

I thought the experience was like a powerful lesson from nature that cleansed a part of me ...and now renewed at the ground level, I knew I was pleased that I found the inner strength to finish the hike despite all the challenges of the weather.

Initially, I was not really looking forward to weathering the storm, but was glad that I did. The experience reminded me of the inner strengths we can call on when needed. Each of us has a wealth of inner strengths that reveal themselves when we get into life's predicaments.

I looked down at my hiking boots clotted with pounds of mud and mused, *real women don't wear glass slippers.*

CHAPTER TWELVE

STORY POEMS

Our life experiences are often revealed in our poetry. These Story Poems were born from my experiences. Perhaps each poem brings some understanding to help our own lives.

CRACKS OF LIGHT

I was injured in a serious auto accident, and I recalled this moment two kind men stood next to me as I lay on the ground waiting for the ambulance to arrive.

"You'll be fine," they said.

Both strangers nodded in unison.

I knew it was a lie, even then.

I saw the fear in their eyes

As they turned away from me.

I tried to move but could not

I felt myself floating upward

Somehow like my body

No longer belonged to me.

Distant arriving sirens wailed

Becoming louder and louder

As each moment ticked away-

Like waiting for a sentence.

Rain began falling on my face.

It was cool, somehow even soothing.

But their faces still haunted me-

Something unspoken in their eyes.

I never saw my face until later

When the doctors gave me

The walker I said I didn't need.

I lied to myself to stay sane.

Nothing seemed the same now.

I felt like a menopausal teen.

Erratic, unpredictable, unstable.

Unable to focus, function, think.

It took a long time before
Someone found my head injury.
Then began the long process
Of building a new self.

"Can't go back," I told myself.
But how I longed for yesterday
When I could float many projects
And delighted in daily challenges.

Now I struggled for words
To make a simple sentence.
And hid from familiar faces
That had no meaning now.

The scars on my body healed faster
Than my broken brain and heart.
I held such sadness deep inside
For so many unknown reasons.

But finally, little cracks of light

Began finding their way inside me

And I took a deepening breath

And set free some of my longings.

It didn't happen overnight, but

Rather inch by inch I found myself

Building other nurturing skills

To help me create new parts of me.

I am grateful for the process.

Proud of help I have received.

So much of what was taken long ago

Recycled to me astoundingly beautiful.

Rebuilt through many cracks of light

My inside beauty growing even brighter.

My gratitude to those who helped me

Heal cracks from that moment in time.

———————————————

HEART OF THE WIND

Solo backpacking in Colorado one time, I sat and reflected upon my childhood. It stirred a desire to return to my childhood home.

I listen to the heart of the wind

For a message calling me home.

Home nurtured my young loved life

Where I baptized my soul complete.

Made a map for my human heart

To remember peace and safety.

Its' memories sustain me

When whirlwinds dance.

The heart of the wind whispers

Yet I cannot hear what it says.

What ghosts lurk in this place?

So vast it does not contain me

My heart struggles to stay open

While the wind whips through me.

I grasp for that invisible home—

Nameless, rich, deep, unseen.

Even though I tell myself

That I carry it with me,

The emptiness I feel reminds me

Of my longing to go home.

A WALK IN THE SHADOWS

I thought when it came time to leave my body and become spirit, I imagine what thoughts would flit through my mind at that moment.

My turn will come

to walk into the unknown

Leaving shadow memories

of the ones I once knew.

I'll turn and in the fading day

I'll disappear into the night.

There is but a moment between it

Beyond the bend and boundaries

Unknown and yet surrendering to all

There I'll carry history in my head

And the lightness in my soul.

But so far I stay and long to learn

More about those deepening thoughts

I have not yet embraced.

So my clinging keeps me here.

Sometimes there is a moment in time,

When I think that all is well

And that I will remember

How to live outside the grace of time;

But, then I find myself forgetting

All that I have promised me

About that special someplace

Where love is remembered well

And lives inside us all.

A secret place that few remember

And fewer yet take time to visit again.

A place of rapture embraced well

By those with awakened hearts.

———————————

RAZOR'S EDGE

This was written for a friend who was having a difficult time. Many of his deep feelings were kept inside of him as he gallantly tried to understand their deeper meaning.

Your tears speak
what your heart cannot.

The brave soul
walks the Razor's Edge
to live authentically.

Such devotion invites vulnerability.
In hiding nothing,
You invite me
to find my freedom
And belonging,

Annemarie Eveland

not longing.

ANGEL EYES

When I became a Hospice volunteer, I was assigned to a petite special Russian lady. Her cherub face and bright sparkling eyes greeted me each time I arrived on my visits to her. In her passing, I was moved to write this poem for her service.

      Bright and sparkling, shining true
      I look down into the eyes of you.
      With gifts of love, back they shine;
      Cheerful still thru mirrors of time.

      I hear some history now and then
      But who you *are* is what you lend.
      It counts less where you've been,
      For what you bring is what you send.

      The lines of hard work on your face

Matter not, for what *you* embrace
Is grander than what's fit for kings.
'Tis wealth of humans that you sing.

I see that life line in your soul
Is *your* sunshine– a gifted goal.
Your eyes reveal a spirit window
Radiating love to those you know.

You speak my name many times,
In communications cherished fine
"You're so thoughtful, you're so kind,"
"Annemarie!" your words then chime.

Little gestures from my helping hands
You genuinely notice such little things-
For just a blanket, a drink or a touch
You profusely thank me very much!"

So, these words come back from me,
For in *you*, Angel Eyes I see!

FOREST FIRES IN MY MOUNTAIN VILLAGE

Every year in the mountain towns, there is Fire Season. Before it arrives, residents clean up their yards and cut back all that will fuel fire. But even with all our efforts, we cannot control nature. This poem recalls a time when I was on high alert to vacate my home. All was subject to the current fire, the winds, the lack of humidity and fate.

———————————

Over this Mogollon Rim, day is breaking.

From my home atop a mountainside,

I see the summer sun has parched this land.

Warm gusty breezes move the ponderosa treetops

Warning of another danger

Little or no rain has come last night

To soothe these brown mountainsides.

Anxiously, I listen to the radio
For messages of a pending evacuation.
I don't want to leave my home in the dark.

The red skies last night kept me awake
Their flames licking fiercely
at the cold black night.

Down the hillside from where I live
I see forest fighters being trucked in.
Working dozers acting importantly loud.

Heavy equipment charges in to thin pine forests
Moaning like metal giant shadows
crawling through the still standing trees.

Somewhere in this valley I hear a cow moaning
For reasons still unknown.
Dogs make their marks audibly sharp

And humming birds are determinedly absent.

The sky becomes a surreal orange now
Not a hint of a cloud, not a whisper of rain.

Everything is covered with gray powder-dust
floating ashes from the fires beyond.

I swallow hard; my throat too is parched.
I wonder about those ancient ones of long ago
Who lived here before we came
and claimed it.
Did they thirst also?
Or was it moist and cool and green?

A streak of sunlight races down the distant mountains.
I inhale and look at the beauty unveiling itself now.

there is a faint hint of moisture in the air.

The distant awesome Mogollon Rim

seems relieved somehow.

A small relief passes through me.

No more important ingredient than the stalling rains.

Then as quickly, the alarm is turned off.

Safe again!

I can stay home.

WHEN I SEE YOU

A friend was expanding in being more open, and I wanted to appreciate her willingness to grow and share.

I see you as a gift of great affection.

I see you as one who loves—

In practical caring ways,

Expressing yourself best in moments

Which hold visions greater than today.

I find you reaching for messages

Written beyond tomorrow's dreams.

I see there is so much more to you

Than all the places you have been.

Yet, tucked inside your heart-
I see a child curling up inside
Fiercely holding onto freedom.
It's the part of you no one knows,
And where even I dare not go.

And yet, I know -I am certain
That the heart you hold within
would make the heavens shudder
And let dancing angels sing.

So, it is possible that tomorrow
When the night has laid to rest.
Those things that made you hide;
Will fly in morning's light?

And with new feelings that are true,
The gentler open parts of you
Will greet the bright new day
With great affection too.

AN ISSUE OF GREATNESS

Although we share deeply with some special people in our lives, there is always that deeper place only each person can visit and know. I saw this as true for a friend of mine.

There is *that* part of you

but there I cannot go,

it is so intrinsic to you

that only you can know.

It's a map of human heart

a vision without the eye,

yet so great it is a love

I find it in you and I.

I cannot give it to you

and you can't give to me.

The only way we know it's rare

is by the ways we share.

Unlike the streams of late daylight

or morning's breath of warmth

we see only how it glows

from each one's slice of life.

So when you feel alone

and when it's dark at day

just remember this secret

and you'll find your way.

For on that path I will stand

and wait and wait for you

for all you are is also me

and together we will renew

As miracles of special light

that beams from heart to heart

In all we do and think and say

to share daily in joyful ways.

———————————

WATER'S EDGE

Once when I was away from my love, the ocean reminded me that he was just a thought away.

My heart sank at the water's edge

and stretched across

the many miles of land

separating my holding you.

The returning waves

carried with them

my longing feelings

brought back through

geographic boundaries.

It was in this moment,

I drew you near to me

and felt that time and space

are never measures

of our closeness.

They are reminders

of my heart reaching out

again and again

to be touched

by your distant love.

———————————————

WINTER SECRETS

When we are having some doubt about our ability, it is helpful to use the metaphor of a seed in winter.

Like the stillness of this winter snow

I cling tenaciously— deep within

Holding fast what makes me unique

In places no one but I can come.

I am a winter wonder

Listening to quieter words

That my heart can hear me

becoming more assured.

A white and silent space I hold

Yet from your outside gaze

Real Women Don't Wear Glass Slippers

I look like frozen feelings

But inside feel amazed.

The seeds I'm holding now

In spring become my power.

And by my courage to believe

I become a magic flower.

That which brings to others

Radiance; and treasures

the things deep inside of us

that grow like giant towers.

So when you think you're stuck

Just sit and listen in the silence

To that which lives inside of you

As eternal strength of essence.

And in the morning light will come

A special kind of knowing

That comes from your very center

As a powerful seed that's growing.

Other Books by Annemarie Eveland

AT FIRST GLANCE WHAT FACES REVEAL (a self-help book on reading people and understanding ourselves)

KEESHA AND THE RAINBOW PARROT GUIDE (a children's story teaching children about loving themselves and dealing with other children different than them.

KEESHA COMPANION GUIDE BOOK (a companion guidebook for teachers and parents to help children understand the storybook)

BE THE RIPPLE (stories showing how small events in ordinary days can bring lasting insights for a lifetime.)

REACHING FOR THE SUN (Poetry)

WISDOM OF THE HEART (Poetry)

ECHOES FROM THE RIM (Stories by Annemarie and other authors)

UPCOMING

HURRAH FOR HUMANS (Stories that celebrate humanity's courage and kindness)

ABOUT THE AUTHOR
ANNEMARIE EVELAND

Annemarie Eveland lives in a small mountain village in the central Arizona Mountains and travels for work and pleasure.

Her professional background includes consultant in personality profiling for corporate businesses and private individuals. She specializes in reading people through their physical structure and is certified as presenter, trainer and profiler since 1980. Her book *At First Glance, What Faces Reveal* is a self-help book teaching these reading people techniques.

Annemarie's trainings and private sessions empower people to appreciate their own unique gifts and talents, shows them how to deal with difficult people and helps them cherish family and friends.

She is available for public speaking engagements, workshops and private consultations.

Her upcoming book: *Hurrah for Humans,* shares life stories that uplift the human spirit, shows the goodness of humanity and the ability humans have to overcome obstacles and learn deeper truths.

On the personal side:
Annemarie enjoys, traveling,; writing, photography, watercolors, hiking, kayaking, natural healing, quiet contemplation and connecting with people on meaningful levels.

She cherishes family, good friends and is an active community supporter wherever she travels.

Annemarie believes, "We are one in spirit, but expressing ourselves as unique, creative human beings."

Did you enjoy *Real Women Don't Wear Glass Slippers?*

You can find more of Annemarie Eveland's writings at annemarieeveland.wordpress.com.

You can also contact her at:

Hurrah for Humans, LLC
P.O. Box 493
Pine, AZ 85544-0493

Made in the USA
Middletown, DE
27 July 2024

57901777R00066